Albert Thomas

THE ONLY HOPE FOR THE BLACK MAN

The Only Hope For The Black Man
Copyright © 2021 by Albert Thomas

All rights reserved. No part of this publication may be reproduced, distributed, or transmitted in any form or by any means, including photocopying, recording, or other electronic or mechanical methods, without the prior written permission of the publisher or author, except in the case of brief quotations embodied in critical reviews and certain other noncommercial uses permitted by copyright law.

Although every precaution has been taken to verify the accuracy of the information contained herein, the author and publisher assume no responsibility for any errors or omissions. No liability is assumed for damages that may result from the use of information contained within.

ISBN-13: Paperback: 978-1-64749-405-6
              ePub: 978-1-64749-361-5

Printed in the United States of America

GoToPublish LLC
1-888-337-1724
www.gotopublish.com
info@gotopublish.com

A MAN NAMED NOAH HAD THREE SONS. THERE NAMES WERE SHEM, HAM, AND JAPHETH. OUT OF HAM CAME THE BLACK MAN (GEN. 9:18).

Genesis 9:18-29

v18 And the sons of No-ah, that went forth of the ark, were Shem, Ham, and Japheth: and Ham is the father of Ca-na-an.

v19 These are the three sons of No-ah: and of them was the whole earth overspread.

v20 And No-ah began to be an husbandman, and he planted a vineyard:

v21 And he drank of the wine, and was drunken; and was uncovered within his tent.

V22 And Ham, the father of Ca-na-an, saw the nakedness of his father, and told his two brethren without.

V23 And Shem and Japheth took a garment, and laid it both upon their shoulders, and went backward, and covered the nakedness of their father; and their faces were backward, and they saw not their father's nakedness.

v24 And No-ah awoke from his wine, and knew what his younger son has done unto him.

v25 And he said, Cursed be Ca-na-an; a servant of servants shall he be unto his brethren.

v26 And he said, Blessed be the Lord God of Shem; and Ca-na-an shall be his servant.

v27 God shall enlarge Ja-pheth, and he shall dwell in the tents of Shem; and Ca-na-an shall be his servant.

v28 And No-ah lived after the flood three hundred and fifty years.

v29 And all the days of No-ah were nine hundred and fifty years: and he died.

The curse spoken on the children of Ham was the beginning of the problem for the black man.

Ham Son of Noah

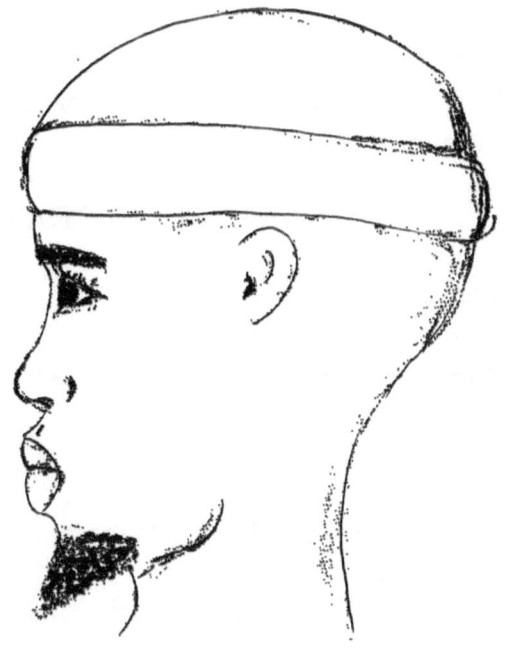

Nimrod the Builder

NIMROD WAS A BLACK MAN

Genesis 10:8-13

v8 And Cush begat Nim-rod: he began to be a mighty one in the earth

v9 He was a mighty hunter before the Lord: wherefore it said, Even as Nim-rod the mighty hunter before the Lord.

v10 And the beginning of his kingdom was Babel, and Erech, and Accad, and Cal-neh, in the land of Shi-nar.

V11 Out of the land went forth Assh-ur, and builded Nin-e-veh and the city Re-ho-both and Ca-lah.

V12 And Re-sen between Nin-e-veh and Ca-lah: the same is a great city.

V13 And Miz-ra-im begat Lu-dim, and A-na-mim, and Le-ha-bim, and Naph-tu-him.

CUSH WAS A SON OF HAM

Genesis 10:14-20

v 14 And Path-ru-sirn and Cas-lu-him, (out of whom came

Phil-is-tim,) and Caph-to-rim.

v 15 And Ca-na-an begat Si-don his firstborn, and Heth,

v 16 And the Jeb-u-site, and the Am-o-rite, and the Gir-ga-site,

v 17 And the Hi-vite, and the Ar-kite, and the Si-nite,

v 18 And the Ar-vad-ite, and the Zem—a-rite, and the I lam-a-thite: and afterward were the families of the Ca-na-an-nites spread abroad.

v 19 And border of the Ca-na-an-ites was from Si-don, as thou comest to Ge-rar, unto Ga-za; as thou goest, unto So-dom, and Go-mor-rah, and Ad-mah, and Ze-bo-im, even unto La-sha.

v 20 These are the sons of Ham, after their families, after their tongues, in their countries, and in their nations.

LSHMAEL—A BLACK MAN

Ishmael was the son of Abraham by an Egyptian woman named Hagar, who was a servant and maid to Sarah. He was banished from his family and disowned, but God didn't forget him because he was a son of Abraham. And later in time we will see what became of his descendants.

Genesis 16:1-16

v1 Now Sarai Abram's wife bare him no children: and she had an handmaid, an Egyptian, whose name was Hagar.

v2 And Sarai said unto Abram, Behold now, the Lord hath restrained me from bearing: I pray thee, go in unto my handmaid; it may be that I may obtained children by her. And Abram hearkened to the voice of Sarai.

Ishmael

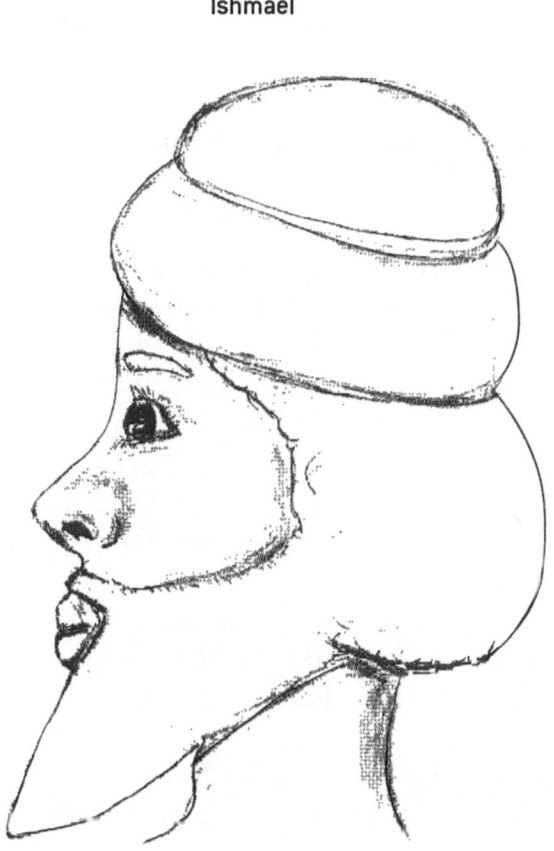

v3 And Sarai Abram's wife took Hagar her maid the Egyptian, after Abram had dwelt ten years in the land of Canaan, and gave her to her husband Abram to be his wife.

v4 And he went in unto Hagar, and she conceived: and when she saw that she had conceived, her mistress was despised in her eyes.

v5 And Sarai said unto Abram, My wrong be upon thee: I have given my maid into thou bosom; and when she saw that she had conceived, I was despised in her eyes: the Lord judge between me and thee.

v6 But Abram said unto Sarai, Behold, thy maid is in thy hands; do to her as it pleaseth thee. And when Sarai dealt hardly with her, she fled from her face.

v7 And the angel of the Lord found her by a fountain of water in the wilderness, by the fountain in the way to Shur.

v8 And he said, Hagar, Sarai's maid, whence camest thou? And wither wilt thou go? And she said, I flee from the face of my mistress Sarai.

v9 And the angel of the Lord said unto her, Return to thy mistress, and submit thyself under her hands.

v10 And the angel of the Lord said unto her, I will multiply thy seed exceedingly, that it shall not be numbered for multitude.

v11 And the angel of the Lord said unto her, Behold, thou art with child, and shalt bear a son, and shalt call his name Ishmael; because the Lord hath heard thy affliction.

V12 And he will be a wild man; his hand will be against every man, and every man's hand against him; and he shall dwell in the presence of all his brethren.

v13 And she called the name of the Lord that spoke unto her, Thou God seest me: for she said, Have I also here looked after him that seeth me?

v14 Wherefore the well was called Beer—la—hai-roi; behold, ll is between Ka—desh and Be-red.

v15 And Hagar bare Abram a son: and Abram called his sons name, which Hagar bare, Ishmael.

v16 And Abram was fourscore and six years old, and Hagar bare Ishmael to Abram.

Pharaoh Rameses II

PHARAOH (RAMESES LL)

He was a black man, who was an Egyptian ruler at the time of Moses. This man God made an example of to deliver the Israelites out of bondage. Exodus 14:1-31

v1 And the Lord spake unto Moses, saying,

v2 Speak unto the children of Is-ra-el, that they turn and encamp before Pi-ha-hi-roth, between Mig-dol and the sea, over against Ba-al-ze—phon: before it shall ye encamp by the sea.

v3 For Pha-raoh will say of the children of Is-ra-el, They are entangled in the land, the wilderness hath shut them in.

v4 And I will harden Pha-raoh's heart, that he shall follow after them: and I will be honoured upon Pha-raoh, and upon all his host; that the Egyptians may know that l am the Lord. And they did so.

v5 And it was told the king of E-gypt that the people fled: and the heart of Pharaoh and of his servants was turned against the people, and they said, Why have we done this, that we have let ls-ra-el go from serving us?

v6 And he made ready his chariot, and took his people with him:

v7 And he took six hundred chosen chariots, and all the chariots of E-gypt, and captains over every one of them.

v8 And the Lord hardened the heart of Pharaoh king of E-gypt, and he pursued after the children of Is-ra-el: and the children of Is-ra-el went out with an high hand.

v9 But the E-gyp-tians pursued after them, all the horses and chariots of Pharaoh, and his horsemen, and his army, and overtook them encamping by the sea, beside Pi-ha-hi-roth, before Ba-al-ze-phon.

v10 And when Pharaoh drew nigh, the children of Is-ra-el lifted up their eyes, and behold, the E-gyp-tians marched after them; and they were sore afraid: and the children of Is-ra-el cried out unto the Lord.

v11 And they said unto Moses, Because they were no graves in E-gypt, hast thou taken us away to die in the wilderness? wherefore hast thou dealt thus with us, to carry us forth out of E-gypt?

v12 Is this not the word that we did tell thee in E-gypt, saying, Let us alone, that we may serve the E-gyp-tians? For it had been better for us to serve the E-gyp-tians, than that we should die in the wilderness.

v13 And Moses said unto the people, Fear ye not, stand still, and see the salvation of the Lord, which he will show to you today: for the

E-gyp-tians whom ye have seen today, ye shall see them again no more for ever.

v14 The Lord shall fight for you, and ye shall hold your peace.

v15 And the Lord said unto Moses, Wherefore criest thou unto me? Speak unto the children of Israel, that they go forward:

v 16 But lift thou up thy rod, and stretch out thine hand over the sea, and divide it: and the children of Israel shall go on dry ground through the midst of the sea.

v17 And I, behold, I will harden the hearts of the Egyptians, and they shall follow them: and I will get me honour upon Pharaoh, and upon all his host, upon his chariots, and upon his horsemen.

v18 And the Egyptians shall know that l am the Lord, when I have gotten me honour upon Pharaoh, upon hischariots, and upon his horsemen.

v19 And the angel of God, which went before the camp of lsrael, removed and went behind them; and the pillar of the cloud went from before their face, and stood behind them:

v20 And it came between the camp of the Egyptians and the camp of the Israel; and it was a cloud and darkness to

them, but it gave light by night to these: so that the onet-.|me not near the other all the night.

v21 And Moses stretched out his hand over the sea; and the Lord caused the sea to go back by a strong east wind all that night, and made the sea dry land, and the waters were divided.

v22 And the children of Israel went into the midst of the sea upon the dry ground: and the waters were a wall unto them on their right hand, and on their left.

v23 And the Egyptians pursued and went in after them into the midst of the sea, all Pharaoh's horses, his chariots, and his horsemen.

v24 And it came to pass, in the morning watch the Lord looked unto the host of the Egyptians through the pillar of fire and of cloud, and troubled the host of the Egyptians,

v25 And took off their chariot wheels, that they drave them heavily: So that the Egyptians said, "Let us flee from the face of Israel, for the Lord fighteth for them against the Egyptians."

v26 And the Lord said unto Moses, Stretch out thine hand over the sea, that the water may come again upon the Egyptians, upon their chariots, and upon their horsemen."

v27 And Moses stretched forth his hand over the sea, and the sea returned to his strength when the morning appeared. And the Egyptians fled against it; and the Lord overthrew the Egyptians in the midst of the sea.

v28 And the waters returned, and covered the chariots, and the horsemen, and all host of Pharaoh that came into the sea after them; there remained not so much as one of them.

v29 But the children of Israel walked upon dry land in the midst of the sea; and the waters were a wall unto them on their right hand, and on their left.

v30 Thus the Lord saved Israel that day out of the hand of the Egyptians, and Israel saw the Egyptians dead upon the seashore.

v31 And Israel saw the great work which the Lord did upon the Egyptians; and the people feared the Lord, and believed the Lord and in his servant Moses.

At the time, God delivered the children of Israel out of Egyptian bondage. There were other people that tagged along and became apart of the Jewish society; some of them were Egyptians. Therefore, there were mixed nationalities among the people of God. Some of them became snares and caused the children of Israel to stumble. Moses himself married an Ethiopian woman. So there were black people mingled in with Israelites even until the time of Hitler, who set out to destroy all blacks and Jews because he couldn't be sure of what nationality they were. He was a God-hater; therefore, he set out to destroy the people of God.

GOLIATH: THE GIANT

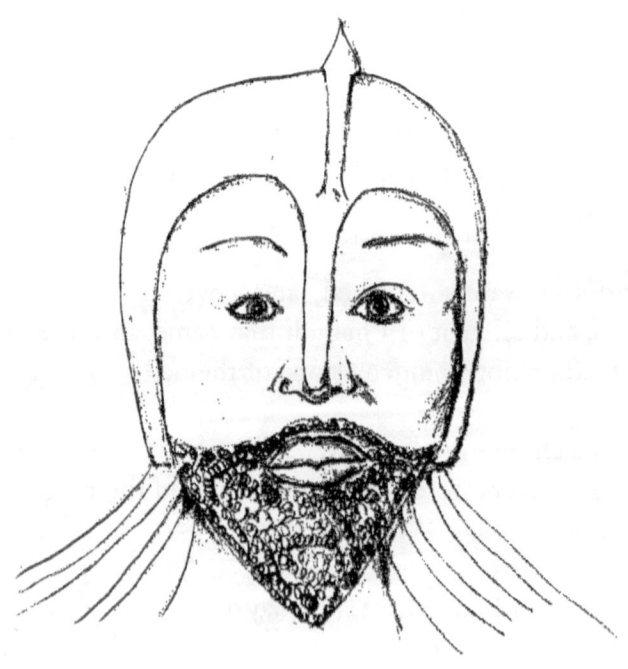

Goliath the Giant

Goliath was a black man who was a Philistine (the Philistine were descendants of Ham). He stood up against the armies of Israel (God's chosen people) and was destroyed. He also had four brothers who were giants. All of which were destroyed by King David's mighty men. One of the giants had six fingers on each hand and six toes on each foot.

1 Samuel 17:41-53

v41 And the Philistine came on and drew near unto David; and the man that bare the shield went before him.

v42 And when the Philistine looked about, and saw David, he disdained him, for he was but a youth, and ruddy, and of a fair countenance.

v43 And the Philistine said unto David, "Am I a dog, that thou comest to me with staves?" And the Philistine cursed David by his gods.

v44 And the Philistine said to David, Come to me, and I will give thy flesh unto the fowls of the air, and to the beasts of the field."

v45 Then said David, to the Philistine, Thou come to me with a sword, and with a spear, and with a shield: but I but I come to thee in the name of the Lord of hosts, the God of the armies of Israel, whom thou has defied.

v46 This day will the Lord deliver thee into my hand; and I will smite thee, take thine head from thee; and I will give the carcases of the host of the Philistines this day unto the fowls of the air, and to the wild beasts of the earth; that all the earth may know that there is a God in Israel.

v47 And that all this assembly may know that the Lord saveth not with sword and spear: for the battle is the Lord's, and he will give you into our hand."

v48 And it came to pass, when the Philistine arose, and came and drew nigh to meet David, that David hasted, and ran toward the army to meet the Philistine.

v49 And David put his hand in his bag, and took hence a stone, and slang it, and smote the Philistine in his forehead, that the stone sunk into his forehead, and he fell upon his face to the earth.

v50 So David prevailed over the Philistine with a sling and with a stone, and smote the Philistine, and slew him. But there was no sword in the hand of David.

v51 Therefore David ran, and stood upon the Philistine, and took his sword, and drew it out of the sheath thereof, and slew him, and cut off his head therewith. And when the Philistines saw that their champion was dead, they fled.

v52 And the men of Israel and Judah arose, and shouted, and pursued the Philistines, until thou come to the valley and to the gates of Ekron. And the wounded of the Philistines fell down by the way to Sha-a-ra-im, even unto Gath, and unto Ekron.

v53 And the children of Israel returned from chasing after the Philistines and they spoiled their tents.

JOAB – THE WARRIOR AND CHIEF

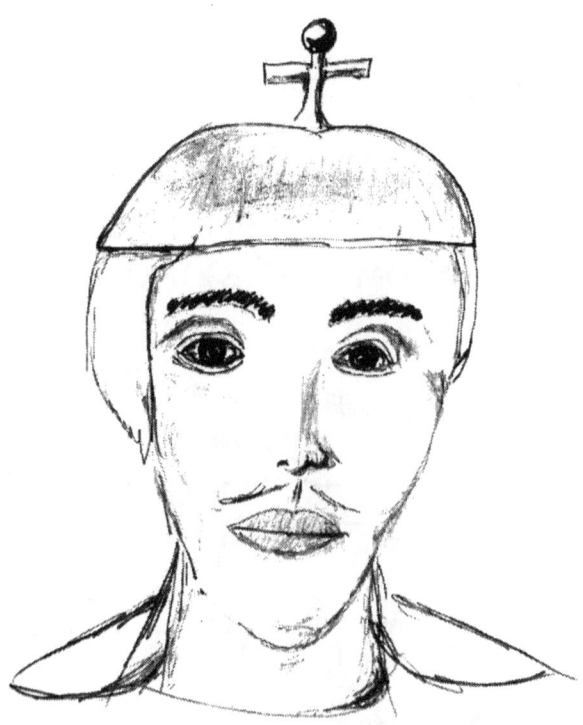

He was a black man who was a great asset to King David thought-out his reign as king but had issues among himself that he couldn't overcome.

In his last days, King Solomon dealt him with a harsh curse.

1 Kings 2:31-33

v31 And the king said unto him, Do as he hath said, and fall upon him, and bury him; that thou mayest take away the innocent blood, which Joab shed, from me, and from the house of my father.

v32 And the Lord shall return his blood upon his own head, who fell upon two men more righteous and better that he, and slew them with the sword, my father David not knowing thereof, to wit, Ab-ner the son of Ner, captain of the host of Israel, and Amasa the son of Je-ther, captain of the host of Judah.

v33 Their blood shall therefore return upon the head of Joab and upon the head of his seed forever: but upon David, and upon his seed, and upon his house, and upon his throne, shall there be peace for ever from the Lord.

SOLOMON THE KING

King Solomon, a black man, the son of King David, the Lord's psalmist, had a black mother. This man prayed a prayer that impressed God so, that he made him the wisest king that ever lived, as well as the richest.

1 Kings 3:6-15

v6 And Solomon said, Thou hast shewed unto thy servant David my father great mercy, according as he walked before thee in truth, and in righteousness, and in uprightness of heart with thee; and thou has kept for him this great kindness, that thou hast given him a son to sit on his throne, as it is this day.

v7 And now, O Lord my God, thou hast made thy servant king instead of David my father: and I am but a little child: I know not how to go out or come in.

v8 And thy servant is in the midst of thy people which thou hast chosen, a great people, that cannot be numbered nor counted for multitude.

v9 Give therefore thy servant an understanding heart to judge thy people, that I may discern between good and bad: for who is able to judge this thy so great a people?

v10 And the speech pleased the Lord, that Solomon had asked this thing.

v11 And God said unto him, Because thou hast asked this thing, and hast not asked for thyself long life, neither hast asked riches for thyself, nor hast asked the life of thine enemies; but hast asked for thyself understanding to discern judgment;

v12 Behold, I have done according to thy words: I have given thee a wise and an understanding heart; so that there was none like thee before thee, neither after thee shall any arise like unto thee.

v13 And I have also given thee that which thou hast not asked, both riches, and honour: so that there shall not be any among the kings like unto thee all thy days.

v14 And if thou wilt walk in my ways, to keep my statutes and my commandments, as thy father David did walk, then I will lengthen thy days.

v15 And Solomon awoke, and behold, it was a dream. And he came to Jerusalem, and stood before the ark of the covenant of the Lord, and offered up burnt offerings, and offered peace offerings, and made a fest to all his servants.

THREE SIMONS OF THE BIBLE

SIMON ZELOTES

He was a black man who also was an apostle. He was a Canaanite chosen by Christ. His name will ever be mentioned alongside the others for eternity as one of the twelve apostles of the Lamb.

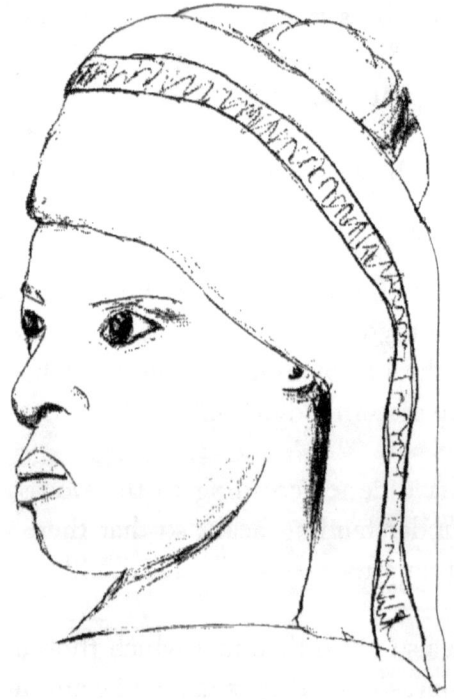

Simon Zelotes

Matthew 10:1-4

v1 And when he called unto him his twelve disciples, he gave them power against unclean spirits, to cast them out, and to heal all manner of sickness and all manner of disease.

v2 Now the names of the twelve apostles are these: the first, Simon, who is called Peter, and Andrew, his brother; James the son of Zebedee, and John his brother;

v3 Philip and Bartholomew; Thomas and Matthew, the publican; James, the son of Alphaeus, and Lebbaeus, whose surname was Thaddaeus;

v4 Simon, the Canaanite, and Judas Iscariot, who also betrayed him.

SIMON OF CYRENE

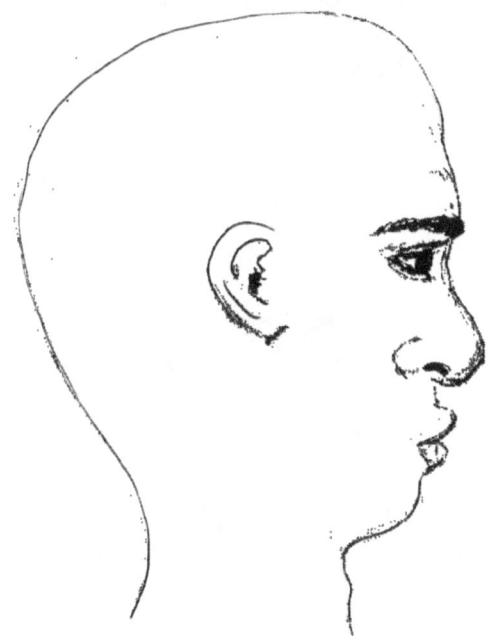

Simon of Cyrene

He was a black man who was compelled to bear the cross of Christ. He nor they knew that this was not an ordinary cross. And the man being crucified was no ordinary man.

Little did anyone know that a black man from that day would help bear the cross of Christ, the effect of sin, and the reproach of sin.

This very well could be the reason why Philip was led by the spirit to bring the Gospel to an Ethiopian eunuch who in turn would spread the Gospel to a whole nation of blacks.

Mark 15:21

v21 And they compel one Simon a Cyrenian, who passed by, coming out of the country, the father of Alexander and Rufus, to bear his cross

SIMON THE SORCERER

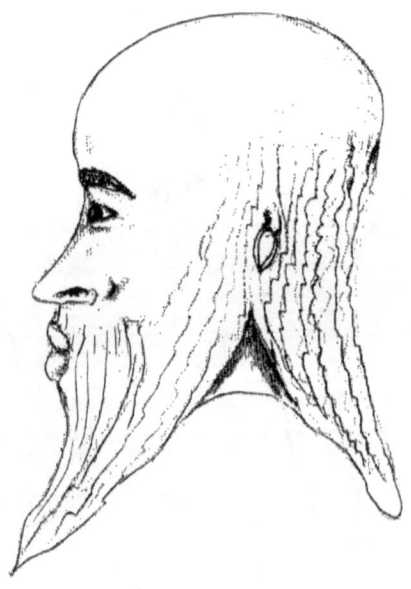

Simon the Sorcerer

He was a black man but desperately wicked. This man through the power of Satan had a whole city under his control.

Acts 8:5-24

v5 Then Philip went down to the city of Samaria, and preached Christ unto them.

v6 And the crowds with one accord gave heed unto those things which Philip spake, hearing and seeing the miracles which he did.

v7 For unclean spirits, crying out with loud voice, came out of many that were possessed, and many taken with palsies, and that were, lame were healed.

v8 And there was great joy in that city.

v9 But there was a certain man, called Simon, which beforetime in the same city used sorcery, and bewitched the people of Samaria, giving out that he himself was some great one:

v10 To whom they all gave heed, from the least to the greatest, saying, This man is the great power of God.

v11 And to him they had regard, because that of long time he had bewitched them with sorceries.

v12 But when they believed Philip preaching the things concerning the kingdom of God, and the name of Jesus Christ, they were baptized, both men and women.

v13 Even Simon himself believed also: and when he was baptized, he continued with Philip, and wondered, beholding the miracles and signs which were done.

v14 Now when the apostles which were at Jerusalem heard that Samaria had received the word of God, they sent to them Peter and John, v15 Who, when they come down, prayed for them that they might receive the Holy Ghost,

v16 (For as yet he was fallen upon none of them: only they were baptized in the name of the Lord Jesus.)

v17 They laid their hands on them, and they received the Holy Ghost.

v18 And when Simon saw that through laying on one of the apostles' hands the Holy Ghost was given, he offered them money,

v19 Saying, Give me also this power, that whomsoever I lay my hands, he may receive the Holy Ghost.

v20 But Peter said unto him, Thy money perish with thee, because thou has thought the gift of God may be purchased with money.

v21 Thou hast neither part nor lot in this matter, for your heart is not right in the sight of God.

v22 Repent therefore of this thy wickedness, and pray God, if perhaps, the thought of thine heart may be forgiven thee.

v23 For I perceive that thou art in the gall of bitterness, and in the bond of iniquity.

v24 Then answered Simon, and said, Pray ye to the Lord for me, that none of these things which ye have spoken come upon me.

THE BIRTH OF THE CHURCH

After these things, the Gospel of the Christ was spread abroad through all the world. So the Gospel was kept alive for many years because of these brave and courageous souls that believed in God through Christ.

Also at the day of Pentecost, many nations and nationalities were gathered together in Jerusalem when the Holy Ghost baptism was given. Many of the people were converted to Christianity and spread the Gospel to their native lands.

Acts 2:1-19

v1 And when the day of Pentecost was fully come, they were all with one accord in one place.

v2 And suddenly there came a sound from heaven as of a rushing mighty wind, and it filled all the house where they were sitting.

v3 And there appeared unto them cloven tongues like as of fire, and it sat upon each of them.

v4 And they were all filled with the Holy Ghost, and began to speak with other tongues, as the Spirit gave them utterance.

v5 And there were dwelling at Jerusalem Jews, devout men, out of every nation under heaven.

v6 Now when this was noised abroad, the multitude came together, and were confounded, because that every man heard them speak in his own language.

v7 And they were all amazed and marveled, saying one to another, Behold are not all these which speak Galilaeans?

v8 And how hear we every man in our own tongue, wherein we were born?

v9 Parthians, and Medes, and Elamites, and the dwellers in Mesopotamia, and in Iudaea, and Cappadocia, in Pontus, and Asia,

v10 Phrygia, and Pamphylia, in Egypt, and in the parts of Libya about Cyrene, and strangers of Rome, Jews and proselytes, v11 Cretes and Arabians, we do hear them speak in our tongues the wonderful works of God.

v12 And they were all amazed, and were in doubt, saying one to another, What meanth this?

v13 Others mocking said, These men are full of new wine.

v14 But Peter, standing up with the eleven, lifted up his voice, and said unto them, Ye men of Judaea and all ye thal dwell at Jerusalem, be this known unto you, and hearken lo my words:

v15 For these are not drunken, as ye suppose, seeing it is but the third hour of the day.

v16 But this is that which was spoken by the prophet Joel;

v17 And it shall come to pass in the last days, saith God, l will pour out of my Spirit upon all flesh: and your sons and your daughters shall prophesy, and your young men shall see visions, and your old men shall dream dreams:

v18 And on my servants and on my handmaidens l will pour out in those days of my Spirit; and they shall prophesy:

v19 And I will shew wonders in heaven above, and signs in the earth beneath; blood, and fire, and vapour of smoke:

THE FIFTH GENERATION

Prov. 30:11-14

v11 There is a generation that curseth their father, and doth not bless their mother v12 There is a generation that are pure in their own eyes, and yet is not washed from filthiness.

v13 There is a generation, O how lofty are their eyes! And their eyelids are lifted up.

v14 There is a generation, whose teeth are as swords, and their jaw teeth as knives, to devour the poor from off the earth and the needy from among men.

THIS GENERATION IS THE FIFTH GENERATION

Psalms 12:1-8

v1 Help, Lord for the godly man ceaseth; for the faithful fail from among the children of men.

v2 They speak vanity every one with his neighbour: with flattering lips and with a double heart do they speak

v3 The Lord shall cut off all flattering lips, and the tongue that speaketh proud things:

v4 Who have said, With our tongues will we prevail; our lips are our own: who is lord over us?

v5 For the oppression of the poor, for the sighing of the needy, now will I arise, saith the Lord; I will set him in safety from him that puffeth at him.

v6 The words of the Lord are pure words: as silver tried in a furnace of earth, purified seven times.

v7 Thou shall keep them, O Lord, thou shalt preserve them from this generation forever.

v8 The wicked walk on every side, when the vilest men are exalted.

WHAT IS THE FIFTH GENERATION?

The 5th Generation is

The generation where the mercy line stops.

The mercy line starts at the righteous person and ends at the fourth generation.

2 Kings 10:30

v30 And the Lord said unto Je-hu, Because thou hast done well in executing that which is right in mine eyes, and hast done unto the house of A-hab according to all that was in mine heart, thy children of the fourth generation shall sit on the throne of Israel.

Psalms 112:1-9

v1 Praise ye the Lord, Blesseth is he that tea reth the Lord, that delighted greatly in his commandments.

v2 His seed shall be mighty upon the earth; the generation of the upright shall be blessed.

v3 Wealth and riches shall be in his house: and his righteousness endureth forever.

v4 Unto the upright there arises light in the darkness: he is gracious, and full of compassion, and righteous.

v5 A good man sheweth favour, and lendeth: he will guide his affairs with discretion.

v6 Surely he shall not be moved forever: the righteous shall be in everlasting remembrance.

v7 He shall not be afraid of evil tiding: his heart is fixed, trusting in the Lord.

v8 His heart is established, he shall not be afraid, until he see his desire upon his enemies.

v9 He hath dispersed, he hath given to the poor:

In the United States of America, in the year of 1865, a president signed into law a proclamation called the Emancipation Proclamation that freed blacks from slavery. His name was Abraham Lincoln.

But before that, many blacks had been converted to Christianity. These people were prayer warriors and prayed for deliverance, just as the children of Israel.

In Bible times, God could not allow his servants that call on him to remain in bondage.

There were also very many Christians that were white that aided in their freedom.

And those who refused to accept God's way and rebelled against the country were defeated. There was much blood shed because of the innocent blood shed of those held in bondage.

And this we learned that all men are created equal and have a right to life, liberty, and happiness.

GENERATION OF 1850-1880

During the generation of 1850-1880, where God's glory and deliverance was shown.

The second generation, 1880-1910, were blessed because of their fathers' commitment to God. The third generation, 1910-1940, God had mercy, and they prospered.

THE FOURTH GENERATION

By the time the fourth generation had come, many of the people of God had turned from God in their hearts and only had a form of godliness. Therefore, God made a last ditch effort to revive the church because He knew the fifth generation was coming. And it was up to the fourth generation to turn their children back to him.

God raised up many leaders out of the third and fourth generation. Great revivals and healing crusades swept the nation. Many people were blessed, delivered, set free, and enjoyed prosperity.

Like Eli, they didn't correct their children and lead them into plain paths. Unlike Abraham, they didn't command their children after them. And many, after being filled with blessings have forsaken God.

So now what we see before us is the fifth generation, and if we don't save the fifth generation, then the sixth generation God will have to destroy.

I guess you can see by now that the only hope for the black man is that he serves God with all his heart all of his days.

Please don't misunderstand, the only hope for any man is Christ but especially the black man, seeing that the odds are against him because of the curse of Noah.

If we must be slaves for someone, let us be slaves for Christ and yet be forever free.

A PRAYER OF REPENTANCE

Lord God Almighty,
I confess that I am lost
And in sin, forgive my sin
In the name of your Son
Jesus Christ. I repent
And ask you to be Lord of
My life.

ABOUT THE AUTHOR

Born Albert McMiller on October 9, 1960, to Lucy McMiller and James Thomas. I grew up in a little town in rural Alabama.

I accepted Christ as Lord and Savior at the age of eighteen.

I later married my wonderful wife, Cynthia, who bore four children, Narlease, Angelica, Keturah, and Albert Gabriel.

Now called by God into the ministry, I decided to write and share some of the things God has revealed to me in these latter days.

ABOUT THE BOOK

Who is this black man, with physical abilities unsurpassed by any other man?

He can be the wisest king and the humblest servant. He can be the greatest architect, a builder, a military leader, and yet the most ruthless cannibal. A man feared so greatly, admired so deeply, loved so passionately, and hated so strongly.

Where did he come from and where is he going?

We will trace his steps and see.

www.ingramcontent.com/pod-product-compliance
Lightning Source LLC
LaVergne TN
LVHW041553060526
838200LV00037B/1271